Editorial Project Manager
Lorin E. Klistoff, M.A.

Editor-in-Chief
Sharon Coan, M.S. Ed.

Cover Artist
Brenda DiAntonis

Art Coordinator
Kevin Barnes

Art Director
CJae Forshay

Imaging
Ralph Olmedo, Jr.
Rosa C. See

Product Manager
Phil Garcia

Publisher
Mary D. Smith, M.S. Ed.

Dr. Fry's Word Sorts

Working with

Phonemes

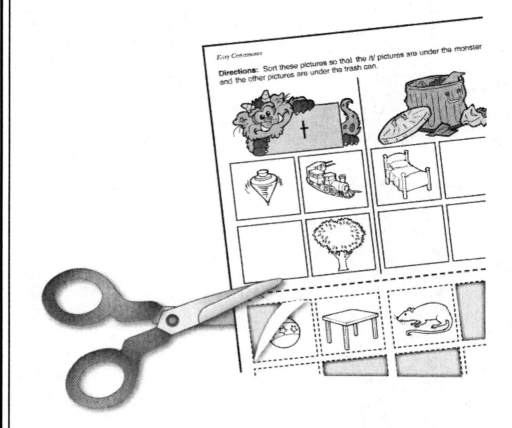

Author

Edward Fry, Ph.D.

Teacher Created Resources, Inc.
6421 Industry Way
Westminster, CA 92683
www.teachercreated.com.
ISBN: 978-0-7439-3712-2
©2003 Teacher Created Resources, Inc.
Reprinted, 2008
Made in U.S.A.

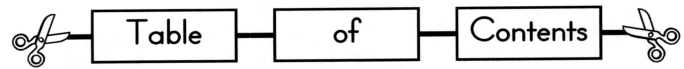

Table of Contents

Introduction

Preparing students for phonics is an important task! *Word Sorts: Working with Phonemes* is a great way for students to manipulate pictures, sounds, and words in a fun and meaningful way! The word sorts contained in this book are for the very beginning reader or early reader. They do not require any reading ability. However, the student who is an early reader can practice reading the words while he or she is sorting. Students may not know how to read all the words, but they will be expected to learn some phoneme awareness and some awareness of the fact that both single letters and digraphs (two-letter combinations) make speech sounds (phonemes). Included in this book are some digraphs that will help students prepare for more formal phonics lessons later. Many of these exercises require the student to hear the difference between sounds at the beginning of words and show the difference by sorting pictures that have similar sounds.

Note, however, that reading pictures is not quite as easy as it sounds, because one student might call a picture a "house" while another student might call the picture a "cabin" or "shack." Hence, for the exercises that show pictures, the teacher should read the words for each picture in the lesson so that the student will call the picture by the correct name. Specific phonics instructions are included at the top of these activity pages.

Other exercises do not use pictures because the sound (phoneme/grapheme correspondence) does not often occur at the beginning of a word, or there are no pictures to illustrate the sound. These exercises use written words. The phonics instructions are also included at the top of these pages.

These word sorts are by no means a complete beginning reading program. However, the word sorts are useful supplemental activities. The activities can be placed at a center. The word sorts can be done individually or in a group setting. The activities can also be used as a quick assessment of each student. In place of cutting the words out, the teacher may elect to have students mark the correct answers with a color. For example, the teacher may ask the students to color all the beginning *t* pictures yellow. It is highly recommended that in conjunction with these word sort activities, students hear stories being read aloud to them and have many opportunities to tell their own stories orally.

Easy Consonants

Phonics Instructions: The letter *t* is a consonant that usually makes the sound /t/, as in *top*. This sound can be made without using the vocal cords or schwa sound at the end. Say /t/, not "tuh." Ask the student to practice the /t/ sound in isolation. Then read aloud the name for each picture: ball, bed, top, train, frog, table, tree, mouse. Have the student sort the pictures.

Student Directions: Cut out the pictures at the bottom of the page. Place the pictures that begin with the /t/ sound under the letter *t*. Place the others under the trash can.

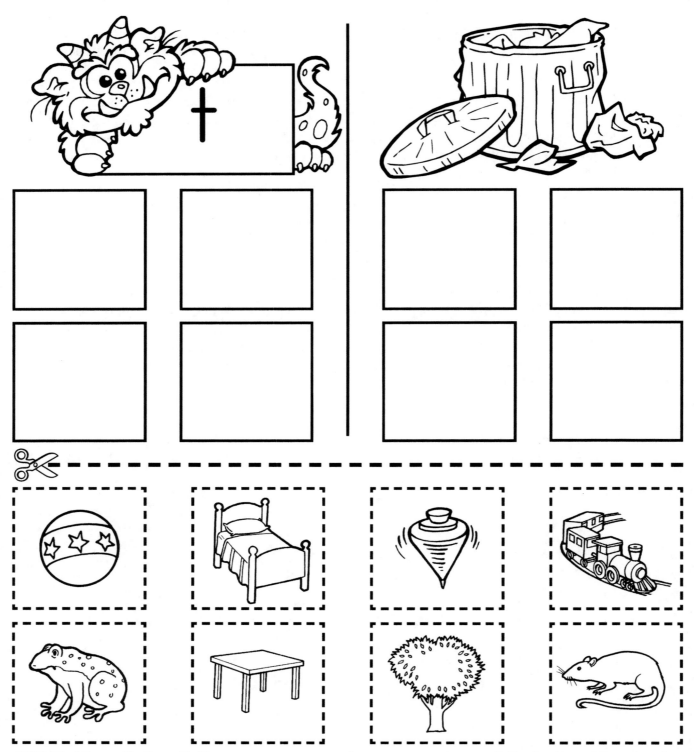

Phonics Instructions: The letter *n* is a consonant that usually makes the sound /n/, as in *no*. This sound always uses the vocal cords, but should not be followed by the schwa sound. Just say /n/, not "nuh." Ask the student to practice the /n/ sound in isolation. Then read aloud the name for each picture: nest, fish, nine, bat, ring, nurse, nickel, jam. Have the student sort the pictures.

Student Directions: Cut out the pictures at the bottom of the page. Place the pictures that begin with the /n/ sound under the letter *n*. Place the others under the trash can.

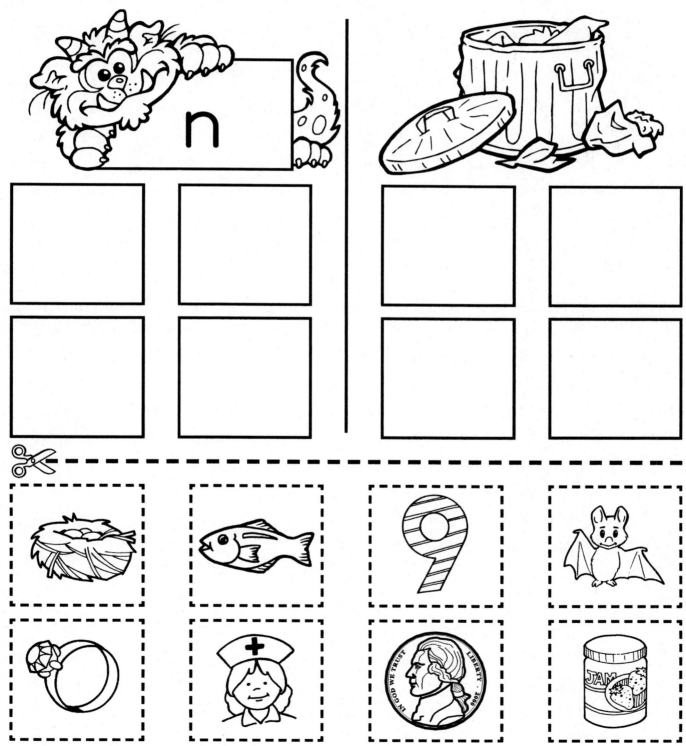

Easy Consonants

Phonics Instructions: The letter *r* is a consonant that usually makes the /r/ sound, as in *red*. This sound always uses the vocal cords, but should not be followed with a schwa at the end. Say /r/, not "ruh." Ask the student to practice the /r/ sound in isolation. Then read aloud the name for each picture: rabbit, fan, ruler, pig, rake, radio, lips, wagon. Have the student sort the pictures.

Student Directions: Cut out the pictures at the bottom of the page. Place the pictures that begin with the /r/ sound under the letter *r*. Place the others under the trash can.

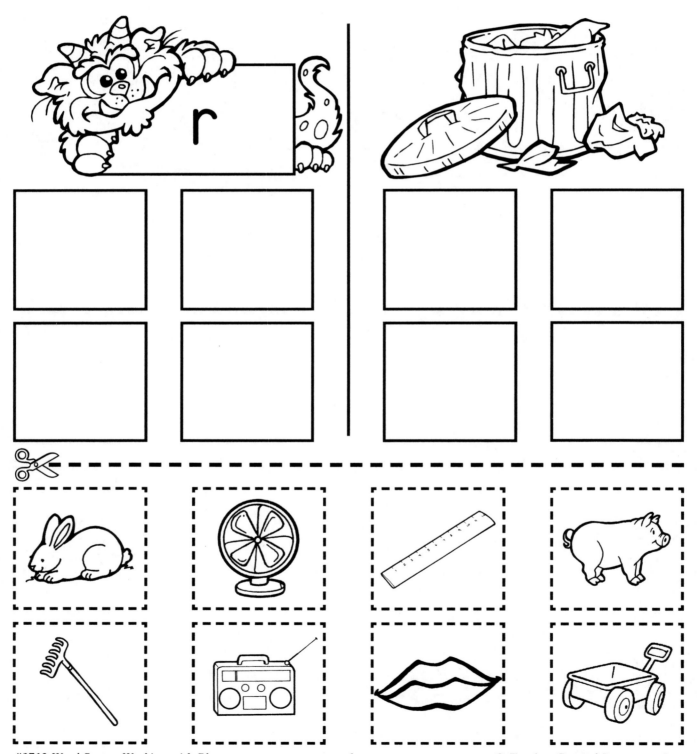

Easy Consonants

Phonics Instructions: The letter *m* is a consonant that usually makes the /m/ sound, as in *man*. This sound always uses the vocal cords, but should not be followed with a schwa at the end. Say /m/, not "muh." Ask the student to practice the /m/ sound in isolation. Then read aloud the name for each picture: man, pencil, goat, moon, meat, mop, block, kite. Have the student sort the pictures.

Student Directions: Cut out the pictures at the bottom of the page. Place the pictures that begin with the /m/ sound under the letter *m*. Place the others under the trash can.

Easy Consonants

Phonics Instructions: The letter *d* is a consonant that usually makes the /d/ sound, as in *dog*. This sound always uses the vocal cords and the schwa, but do not overemphasize the schwa. Ask the student to practice the /d/ sound in isolation. Then read aloud the name for each picture: duck, car, frog, dress, wagon, mask, drum, dog. Have the student sort the pictures.

Student Directions: Cut out the pictures at the bottom of the page. Place the pictures that begin with the /d/ sound under the letter *d*. Place the others under the trash can.

Easy Consonants

Phonics Instructions: The letter *s* is one of the few consonants that has two sounds. The sound /s/, as in *saw,* is the most common. The letter *s* almost always makes this sound at the beginning of a word. This sound can be made without using the vocal cords or the schwa sound at the end. Say /s/, not "suh." Ask the student to practice the /s/ sound in isolation. Then read aloud the name for each picture: sun, watch, saw, cat, sock, star, pig, flower. Have the student sort the pictures.

Student Directions: Cut out the pictures at the bottom of the page. Place the pictures that begin with the /s/ sound under the letter *s*. Place the others under the trash can.

Easy Consonants

Phonics Instructions: The letter *l* is a consonant that usually makes the /l/ sound, as in *look*. This sound always uses the vocal cords but should not be followed with a schwa at the end. Say /l/, not "luh." Ask the student to practice the /l/ sound in isolation. Then read aloud the name of each picture: lamp, key, leaf, table, jar, ladder, letter, house. Have the student sort the pictures.

Student Directions: Cut out the pictures at the bottom of the page. Place the pictures that begin with the /l/ sound under the letter *l*. Place the others under the trash can.

Easy Consonants

Phonics Instructions: The letter *c* usually has the sound of /k/. For example, the *c* in the word *cat* has the sound of /k/. This sound can be made without using the vocal cords or the schwa sound at the end. The letter *c* usually makes the /k/ sound before *a*, *o*, and *u*. Ask the student to practice the /k/ sound in isolation. Then read aloud the name of each picture: cat, rug, vest, cup, ring, glove, car, cow. Have the student sort the pictures.

Student Directions: Cut out the pictures at the bottom of the page. Place the pictures that begin with the /k/ sound under the letter *c*. Place the others under the trash can.

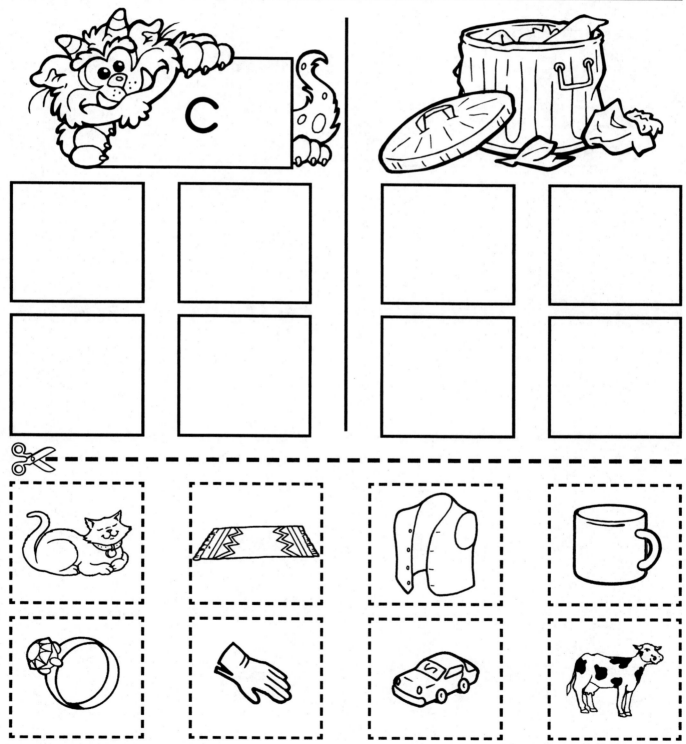

Phonics Instructions: The letter *p* is a consonant that usually has the sound of /p/, as in *pig*. This sound can be made without using the vocal cords or the schwa sound at the end. Say /p/, not "puh." Ask the student to practice the /p/ sound in isolation. Then read aloud the name of each picture: pig, yarn, fire, pencil, paint, penny, brush, vase. Have the student sort the pictures.

Student Directions: Cut out the pictures at the bottom of the page. Place the pictures that begin with the /p/ sound under the letter *p*. Place the others under the trash can.

Easy Consonants

Phonics Instructions: The letter *b* is a consonant that makes the sound of /b/, as in *boy*. This sound uses the vocal cords and the schwa; however, do not overemphasize the schwa. Say /b/, not "buh." Ask the student to practice the /b/ sound in isolation. Then read aloud the name of each picture: book, snake, box, pie, bell, wig, mop, bowl. Have the student sort the pictures.

Student Directions: Cut out the pictures at the bottom of the page. Place the pictures that begin with the /b/ sound under the letter *b*. Place the others under the trash can.

Easy Consonants

Phonics Instructions: The letter *f* is a consonant that almost always makes the sound /f/, as in *fish*. This sound can be made without using the vocal cords or the schwa sound at the end. Say /f/, not "fuh." Ask the student to practice the /f/ sound in isolation. Then read aloud the name of each picture: fish, flower, pizza, bird, saw, fox, bag, fan. Have the student sort the pictures.

Student Directions: Cut out the pictures at the bottom of the page. Place the pictures that begin with the /f/ sound under the letter *f*. Place the others under the trash can.

Phonics Instructions: The letter *v* is a consonant that usually has the sound /v/, as in *very*. This sound always uses the vocal cords but should not be followed with a schwa at the end. Say /v/, not "vuh." Ask the student to practice the /v/ sound in isolation. Then read aloud the name of each picture: vest, comb, vase, shoe, cap, tire, van, violin. Have the student sort the pictures.

Student Directions: Cut out the pictures at the bottom of the page. Place the pictures that begin with the /v/ sound under the letter *v*. Place the others under the trash can.

Phonics Instructions: The letter *a* is a vowel that has several sounds. The short sound of *a*, as in *as*, is the most common and should be taught first. Ask the student to practice the /a/ sound in isolation. Then read aloud the name of each picture: fish, apple, comb, ant, bell, alligator, wig, ax. Have the student sort the pictures.

Student Directions: Cut out the pictures at the bottom of the page. Place the pictures that begin with the short /a/ sound under the letter *a*. Place the others under the trash can.

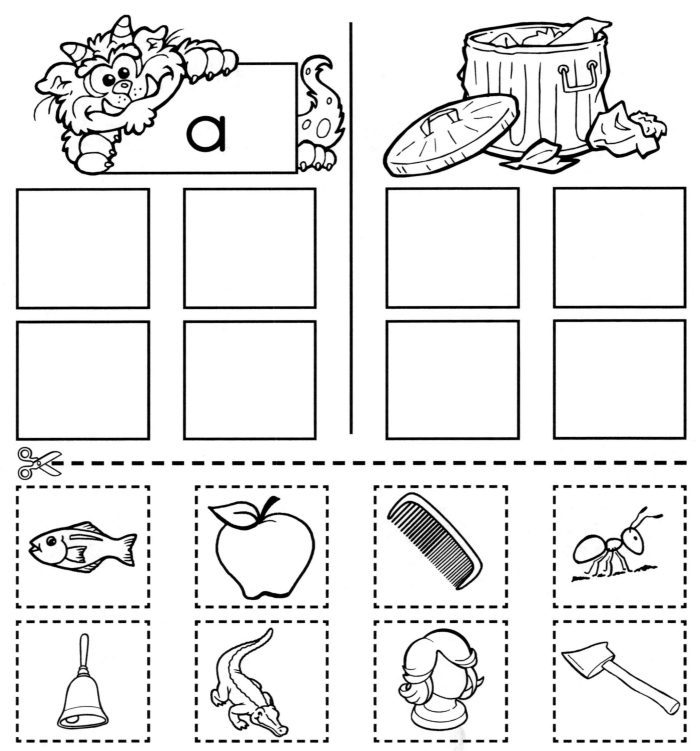

Short Vowels

Phonics Instructions: The letter *e* is a vowel that has several sounds. The short sound of *e*, as in *end*, should be taught first, because it is the most common. Ask the student to practice the short /e/ in isolation. Then read aloud the name of each picture: elephant, moon, duck, eggs, cat, elbow, sun, elf. Have the student sort the pictures.

Student Directions: Cut out the pictures at the bottom of the page. Place the pictures that begin with the short /e/ sound under the letter *e*. Place the others under the trash can.

Short Vowels

Phonics Instructions: The letter *i* is a vowel that has several sounds. The short sound of *i*, as in *is*, should be taught first, because it is the most common. Ask the student to practice the short /i/ sound in isolation. Then read aloud the name of each picture: lamp, igloo, Indian, ball, insect, rake, ink, nurse. Have the student sort the pictures.

Student Directions: Cut out the pictures at the bottom of the page. Place the pictures that begin with the short /i/ sound under the letter *i*. Place the others under the trash can.

Short Vowels

Phonics Instructions: The letter *o* is a vowel that has several sounds. The short sound of *o*, as in *on*, is the most common and should be taught first. Ask the student to practice the short /o/ sound in isolation. Read the name of each picture: ostrich, key, otter, wig, fish, octopus, oxen, bell. Have the student sort the pictures.

Student Directions: Cut out the pictures at the bottom of the page. Place the pictures that begin with the short /o/ sound under the letter *o*. Place the others under the trash can.

Short Vowels

Phonics Instructions: The letter *u* is a vowel that has several sounds. The short sound of *u*, as in *up*, is the most common and should be taught first. Ask the student to practice the short /u/ sound in isolation. Read the name of each picture: umbrella, underwear, kite, fly, moon, undersea, vase, umpire. Have the student sort the pictures.

Student Directions: Cut out the pictures at the bottom of the page. Place the pictures that begin with the short /u/ sound under the letter *u*. Place the others under the trash can.

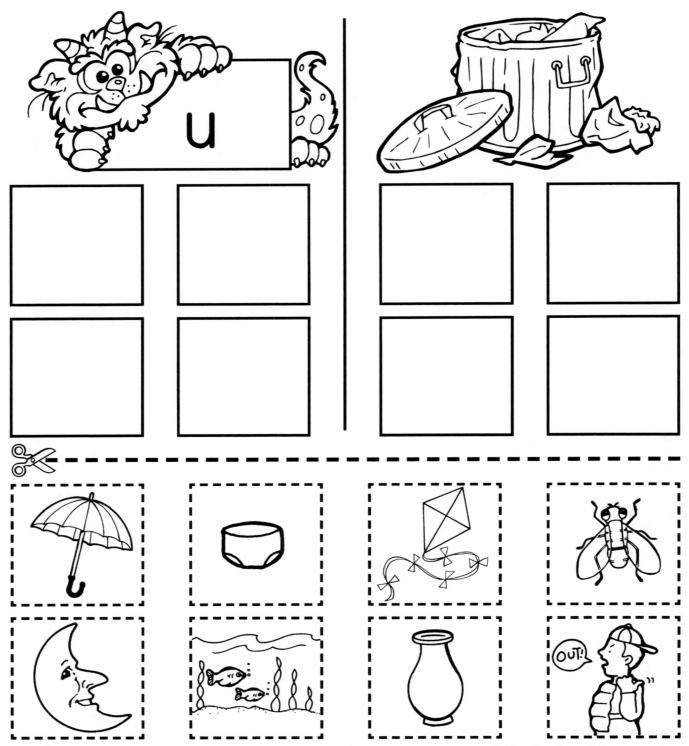

Phonics Instructions: The letter *y* is most frequently a vowel that has the long *e* sound, as in *very*. This is true when *y* is at the end of a word that contains another vowel. Ask the student to practice the long /e/ sound in isolation. Read the words on the page aloud with the student repeating them. Have the student sort the words.

Student Directions: Cut out the words at the bottom of the page. Place the words that begin with the long /e/ sound under the letter *y*. Place the others under the trash can.

Phonics Instructions: The letter *e* at the end of the word that contains another vowel sound is usually silent. This rule is more useful and consistent than the Final "e" Rule, which will be taught later. Read the words aloud with the student repeating them. Have the student sort the words.

Student Directions: Cut out the words at the bottom of the page. Place the words that end with the silent *e* under the letter *e*. Place the others under the trash can.

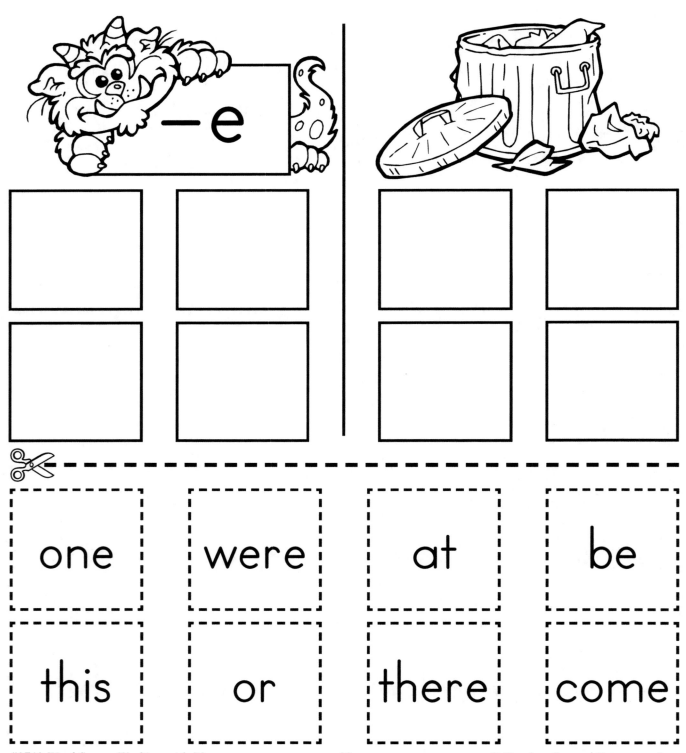

Long Vowels (Final "e" Rule)

Phonics Instructions: The second most common sound of *a* is the long sound, as in *take*. The long *a* is frequently made by placing a silent *e* at the end of the word or syllable. Note the difference between *mad* and *made*. Ask the student to practice the long /ā/. Read aloud the words with the student repeating them. Have the student sort the words.

Student Directions: Cut out the words at the bottom of the page. Place the words with the long *a* sound together under the monster. Place the others under the trash can.

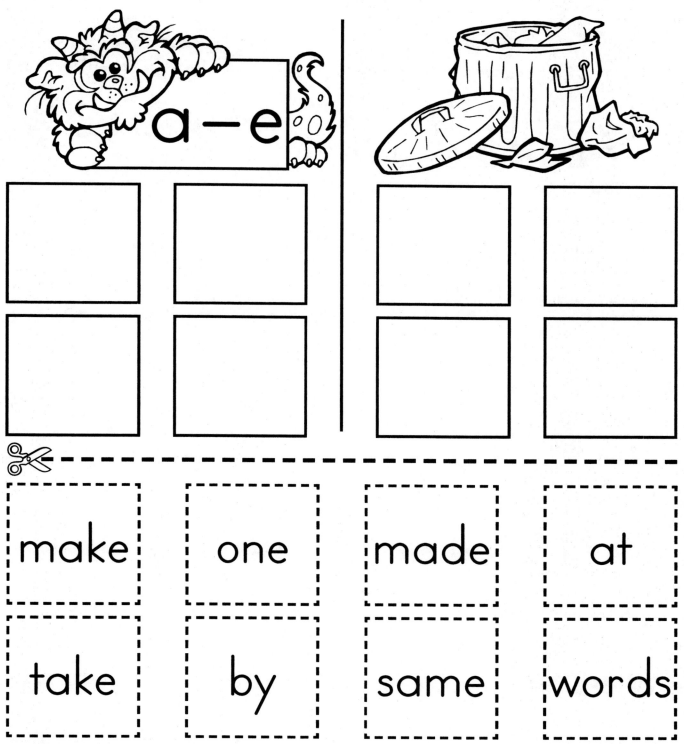

| make | one | made | at |
| take | by | same | words |

Long Vowels (Final "e" Rule)

Phonics Instruction: The second most common sound of *i* is the long sound, as in *like*. The long *i* sound is frequently made by placing a silent *e* at the end of a word. Ask the student to practice the long /ī/ sound in isolation. Read the words aloud with the student repeating them. Have the student sort the words.

Student Directions: Cut out the words at the bottom of the page. Place the words with the long *i* sound together under the monster. Place the others under the trash can.

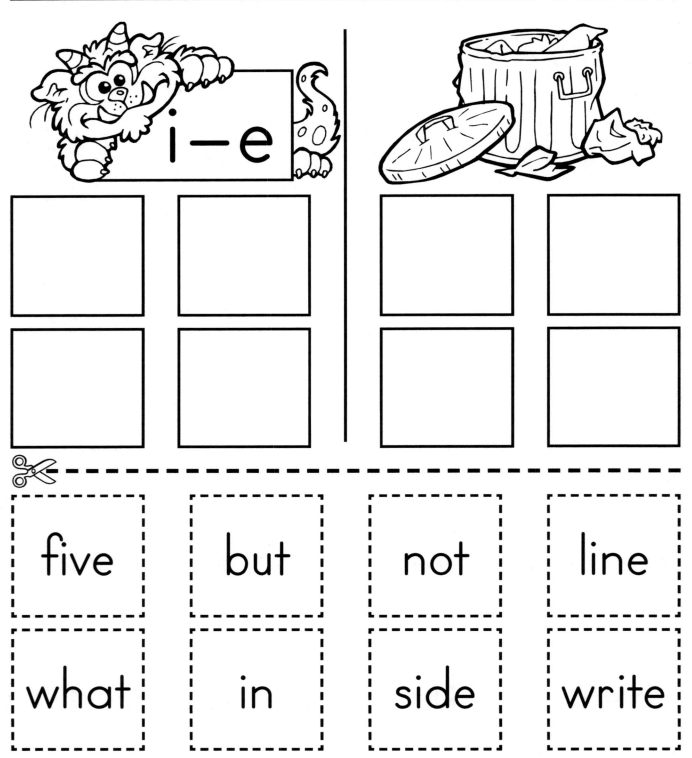

five | but | not | line

what | in | side | write

Long Vowels (Final "e" Rule)

Phonics Instructions: The second most common sound of *o* is the long sound as in *home*. It is frequently made by placing a silent *e* at the end of the word or syllable. Ask the student to practice the long /ō/ sound in isolation. Read the words aloud with the student repeating them. Have the student sort the words.

Student Directions: Cut out the words at the bottom of the page. Place the words with the long *o* sound together under the monster. Place the others under the trash can.

all   bone   were   not

home   hope   we   those

Phonics Instructions: The long sound of *a* is sometimes made by the "Open Syllable Rule," which states that when a syllable ends in a vowel, the vowel is pronounced with the long sound, as in *paper*. Ask the student to practice the long /ā/ sound in isolation. Read the name of each picture: glue, bed, lady, baby, radio, gum, pig, table. Have the student sort the pictures.

Student Directions: Cut out the pictures at the bottom of the page. Place the pictures with the long *a* sound together under the monster. Place the others under the trash can.

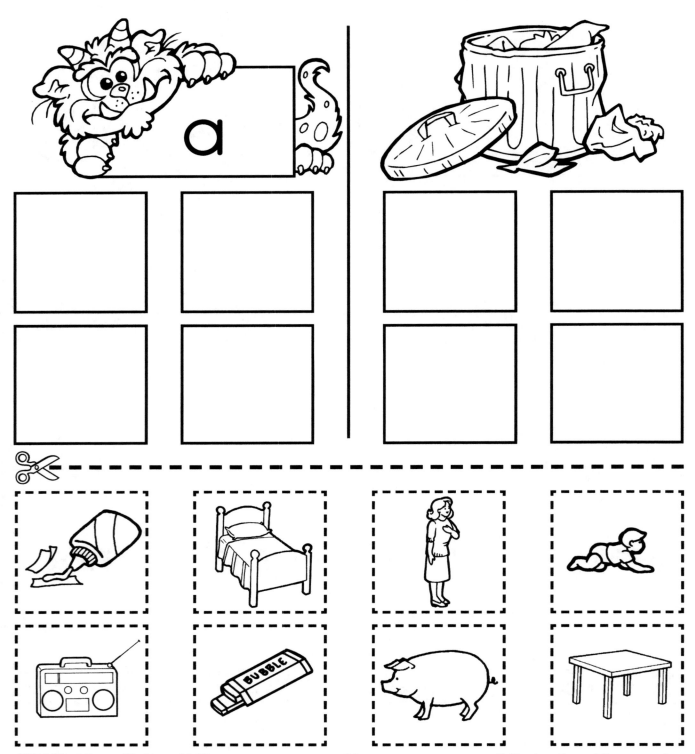

Long Vowels (Open Syllable Rule)

Phonics Instructions: The long sound of *e* is sometimes made by the "Open Syllable Rule," which states that when a syllable ends in a vowel, the vowel is pronounced with the long sound, as in *me*. Ask the student to practice the long /ē/ sound in isolation. Then read the name of each picture: three, box, equal, cat, car, tree, lamp, beehive. Have the student sort the pictures.

Student Directions: Cut out the pictures at the bottom of the page. Place the pictures with the long *e* sound together under the monster. Place the others under the trash can.

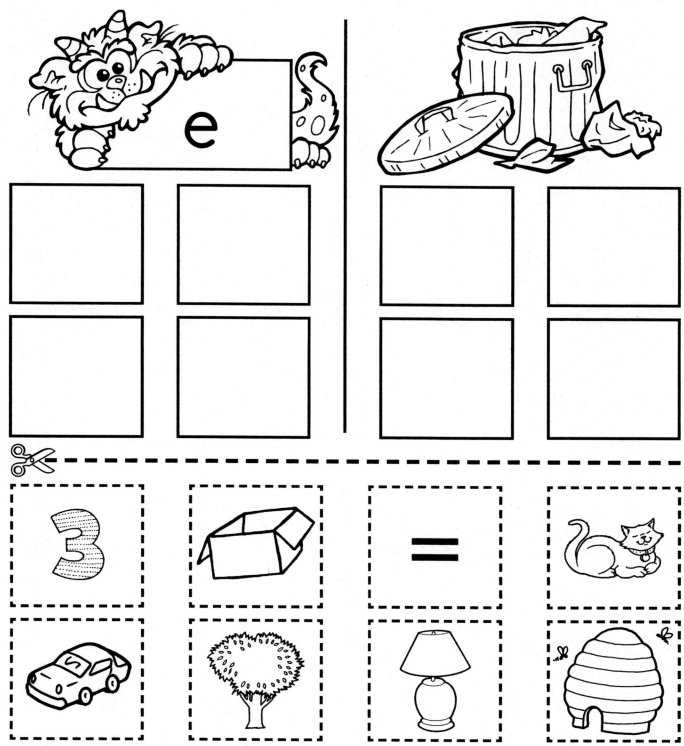

Long Vowels (Open Syllable Rule)

Phonics Instructions: The long sound of *i* is sometimes made by the "Open Syllable Rule," which states that when a syllable ends in a vowel, the vowel is pronounced with the long sound, as in *tiger*. Ask the student to practice the long /ī/ sound in isolation. Then read the name of each picture: duck, tiger, triangle, flag, bicycle, spider, frog, book. Have the student sort the pictures.

Student Directions: Cut out the pictures at the bottom of the page. Place the pictures with the long *i* sound together under the monster. Place the others under the trash can.

Long Vowels (Open Syllable Rule)

Phonics Instructions: The long sound of *o* is sometimes made by the "Open Syllable Rule," which states that when a syllable ends in a vowel, the vowel is pronounced with the long sound, as in *go*. Ask the student to practice the long /ō/ sound in isolation. Then read the name of each picture: ocean, potato, bag, skate, piano, radio, net, scale. Have the student sort the pictures.

Student Directions: Cut out the pictures at the bottom of the page. Place the pictures with the long *o* sound together under the monster. Place the others under the trash can.

Long Vowels (Open Syllable Rule)

Phonics Instructions: The long sound of *u* is sometimes made by the "Open Syllable Rule," which states that when a syllable ends in a vowel, the vowel is pronounced with the long sound, as in *human*. Ask the student to practice the long /yōo/ sound in isolation. Then read the words aloud with the student repeating them. Have the student sort the words.

Student Directions: Cut out the words at the bottom of the page. Place the words with the long *u* sound together under the monster. Place the others under the trash can.

ruler	be	tuba	this
music	have	human	or

Difficult Consonants

Phonics Instructions: The consonant *g* has two sounds. The most common is the /g/ sound as in *good.* It frequently makes this sound before *a, o, u,* and when it is the last letter in a word. This sound uses the vocal cords and the schwa; however, do not overemphasize the schwa. Ask the student to practice the /g/ sound in isolation. Then read the name of each picture: grapes, glass, book, pencil, elephant, tire, gum, girl. Have the student sort the pictures.

Student Directions: Cut out the pictures at the bottom of the page. Place the pictures that begin with the /g/ sound under the letter *g.* Place the others under the trash can.

Difficult Consonants

Phonics Information: The letter *h* is a consonant that usually makes the /h/ sound, as in *hat*. This sound can be made without using the vocal cords or the schwa sound at the end. Say /h/, not "huh." Ask the student to practice the /h/ sound in isolation. Then read the name of each picture: box, horse, hand, tree, home, bat, car, hat. Have the student sort the pictures.

Student Directions: Cut out the pictures at the bottom of the page. Place the pictures that begin with the /h/ sound under the letter *h*. Place the others under the trash can.

Difficult Consonants

Phonics Instructions: The letter *k* is a consonant that usually makes the /k/ sound, as in *kind*. This sound can be made without using the vocal cords or the schwa sound at the end. Say /k/, not "kuh." Ask the student to practice the /k/ sound in isolation. Then read the name of each picture: key, frog, ring, kite, king, drum, jam, kangaroo. Have the student sort the pictures.

Student Directions: Cut out the pictures at the bottom of the page. Place the pictures that begin with the /k/ sound under the letter *k*. Place the others under the trash can.

Difficult Consonants

Phonics Instructions: The letter *w* is a consonant that usually makes the /w/ sound, as in *we*. This sound uses the vocal cords and the schwa. Do not overemphasize the schwa. Say /w/, not "wuh." Ask the student to practice the /w/ sound in isolation. Then read the name of each picture: pig, mask, woman, wagon, wig, watch, penny, fire. Have the student sort the pictures.

Student Directions: Cut out the pictures at the bottom of the page. Place the pictures that begin with the /w/ sound under the letter *w*. Place the others under the trash can.

Phonics Instructions: The letter *j* is a consonant that usually makes the /j/ sound, as in *just*. This sound uses the vocal cords and the schwa. Do not overemphasize the schwa. Ask the student to practice the /j/ sound in isolation. Read the name of each picture: jam, jacket, duck, paint, table, mouse, jar, jacks. Have the student sort the pictures.

Student Directions: Cut out the pictures at the bottom of the page. Place the pictures that begin with the /j/ sound under the letter *j*. Place the others under the trash can.

Difficult Consonants

Phonics Instructions: The letter *x* does not have a sound of its own. The letter *x* usually sounds like /ks/, as in *box*. This sound can be made without using the vocal cords or the schwa sound at the end. The letter *x* is usually found at the end of a word or syllable. Ask the student to practice the /ks/ sound in isolation. Then read the name of each picture: yarn, dog, fox, six, box, ax, elephant, igloo. Have the student sort the pictures.

Student Directions: Cut out the pictures at the bottom of the page. Place the pictures that have the /ks/ sound under the letter *x*. Place the others under the trash can.

Difficult Consonants

Phonics Instructions: The letter *q* is a consonant of relatively low frequency. It always appears with *u*. The combination *qu* makes the /kw/ sound, as in *queen*. Ask the student to practice the /kw/ sound in isolation. Then read the name of each picture: rake, queen, quarter, question, top, quilt, fan, bed. Have the student sort the pictures.

Student Directions: Cut out the pictures at the bottom of the page. Place the pictures that begin with the /kw/ sound under the letters *qu*. Place the others under the trash can.

Phonics Instructions: The letter *z* is a consonant that usually makes the /z/ sound, as in *zoo*. This sound always uses the vocal cords but should not be followed with a schwa at the end. Say /z/, not "zuh." Ask the student to practice the /z/ sound in isolation. Then read the name of each picture: zebra, zero, ring, penny, cup, table, zipper, zucchini. Have the student sort the pictures.

Student Directions: Cut out the pictures at the bottom of the page. Place the pictures that begin with the /z/ sound under the letter *z*. Place the others under the trash can.

Difficult Consonants

Phonics Instructions: When *y* is at the beginning of a word, it makes the /y/ sound, as in *yes*. This uses the vocal cords and the schwa; however, do not overemphasize the schwa. Say /y/, not "yuh." Ask the student to practice the /y/ sound in isolation. Then read the name of each picture: shoe, leaf, yarn, cap, yo-yo, yogurt, yacht, comb. Have the student sort the pictures.

Student Directions: Cut out the pictures at the bottom of the page. Place the pictures that begin with the /y/ sound under the letter *y*. Place the others under the trash can.

Consonant Digraphs

Phonics Instructons: *Th* is a consonant digraph that has two sounds, neither of which is a blend of *t* and *h*. This sound most frequently found in words commonly taught to beginning readers is the voiced *th*, as in *the*. Voiced means that the vocal cords are used in making the *th* sound. It can be made without the schwa sound at the end. Ask the student to practice the voiced /th/ sound in isolation. Then read the words aloud with the student repeating them. Have the student sort the words.

Student Directions: Cut out the words at the bottom of the page. Place the words that begin with the /th/ sound under the letters *th*. Place the others under the trash can.

of

that

and

they

to

this

you

there

Phonics Instructions: The voiceless *th*, as in the word *thin*, does not use the vocal cords. It can be made without the schwa sound at the end. Ask the student to practice the voiceless /th/ sound in isolation. Then read the name of each picture: thimble, cow, thread, vase, thirteen, pie, thumb, mop. Have the student sort the pictures.

Student Directions: Cut out the pictures at the bottom of the page. Place the pictures that begin with the /th/ sound under the letters *th*. Place the others under the trash can.

Consonant Digraphs

Phonics Instructions: The digraph *ch* makes the sound heard at the beginning of the word *child*. It is not a blend of *c* and *h*, but is a unique sound. This sound is voiceless and can be made without the schwa sound at the end. Ask the student to practice the /ch/ sound in isolation. Then read the name of each picture: chair, pencil, cheese, ladder, children, bird, cherries, snake. Have the student sort the pictures.

Student Directions: Cut out the pictures at the bottom of the page. Place the pictures that begin with the /ch/ sound under the letters *ch*. Place the others under the trash can.

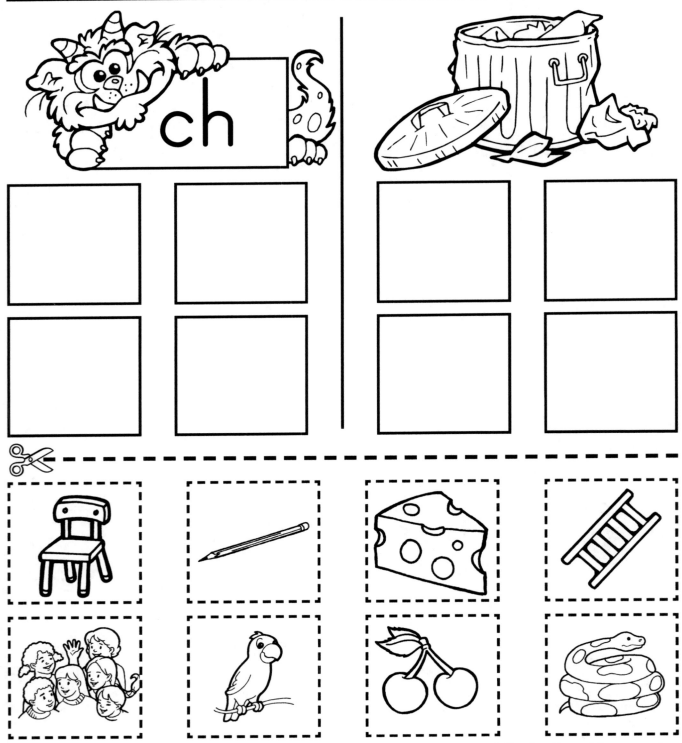

Phonics Instructions: The digraph *sh* makes the sound heard at the beginning of the word *she*. It is not a blend of *s* and *h*, but is a unique sound. This sound is voiceless and can be made without the schwa sound at the end. Ask the student to practice the /sh/ sound in isolation. Then read the name of each picture: shirt, sheep, nickel, lamp, jar, violin, shell, shorts. Have the student sort the pictures.

Student Directions: Cut out the pictures at the bottom of the page. Place the pictures that begin with the /sh/ sound under the letters *sh*. Place the others under the trash can.

Phonics Instructions: The digraph *wh* makes the sound heard at the beginning of the word *when*. It is not a blend of *w* and *h*. It is a unique sound, usually called a consonant digraph, but sometimes referred to as the sound of *h* and *w* blended. This sound is voiceless and can be made without the schwa sound at the end. Ask the student to practice the /hw/ sound in isolation. Then read aloud the name of each picture: apple, book, king, wheel, whistle, whale, wheat, jacket. Have the student sort the pictures.

Student Directions: Cut out the pictures at the bottom of the page. Place the pictures that begin with the /hw/ sound under the letters *wh*. Place the others under the trash can.

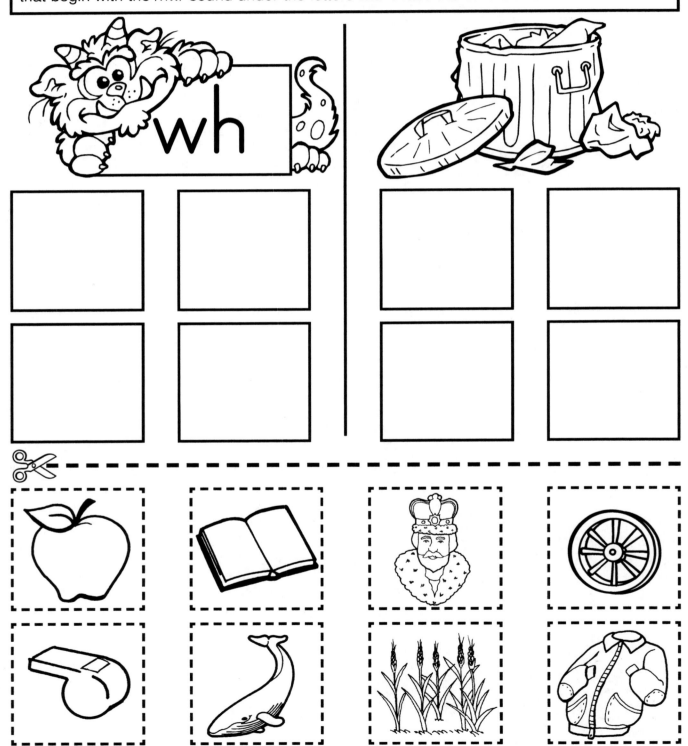

Consonant Second Sounds

Phonics Instructions: The second sound of *c* is the /s/ sound, as in *city*. The letter *c* frequently makes this sound before *i*, *e*, and *y*. This sound can be made without using the vocal cords or the schwa sound at the end. Ask the student to practice the /s/ sound in isolation. Read aloud the words with the student repeating them. Have the student sort the pictures.

Student Directions: Cut out the words at the bottom of the page. Place the words that begin with the /s/ sound under the letter *c*. Place the others under the trash can.

Phonics Instructions: The second sound of *s* is the /z/ sound as in *has*. The sound always uses the vocal cords, but should not be followed with a schwa at the end. The letter *s* tends to make the /z/ sound when it is the final sound in a word or syllable if it is preceded by a voiced sound. The letter *s* makes the /z/ sound in words much more frequently than *z* itself does. Therefore, the most common way to spell the /z/ sound is with *s*. Ask the student to practice making the /z/ sound in isolation. Then read aloud the words with the student repeating them. Have the student sort the words.

Student Directions: Cut out the words at the bottom of the page. Place the words that have the /z/ sound under the letter *s*. Place the others under the trash can.

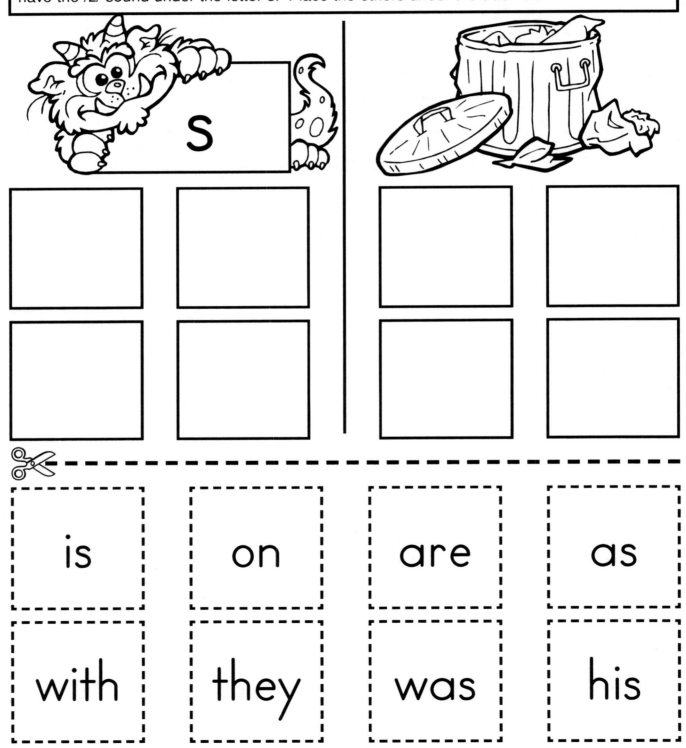

is   on   are   as

with   they   was   his

46

Consonant Second Sounds

Phonics Instructions: The second sound of *g* is the /j/ sound, as in *general*. This /j/ sound of *g* is often made when *g* is followed by *i*, *e*, or *y*. This sound uses the vocal cords and the schwa; however, do not overemphasize the schwa. Ask the student to practice the /j/ sound in isolation. Read the words aloud with the student repeating them. Have the student sort the words.

Student Directions: Cut out the words at the bottom of the page. Place the words that have the /j/ sound under the letter *g*. Place the others under the trash can.

Phonics Instructions: The letter *y* sometimes sounds like long *i*, as in *my*. This is usually when it is at the end of a word that contains no other vowel or when *y* appears in the middle of a word, as in *cyclone*. Ask the student to practice the long /ī/ in isolation. Then read the words aloud with the student repeating them. Have the student sort the words.

Student Directions: Cut out the words at the bottom of the page. Place the words that have the long /ī/ sound under the letter *y*. Place the others under the trash can.

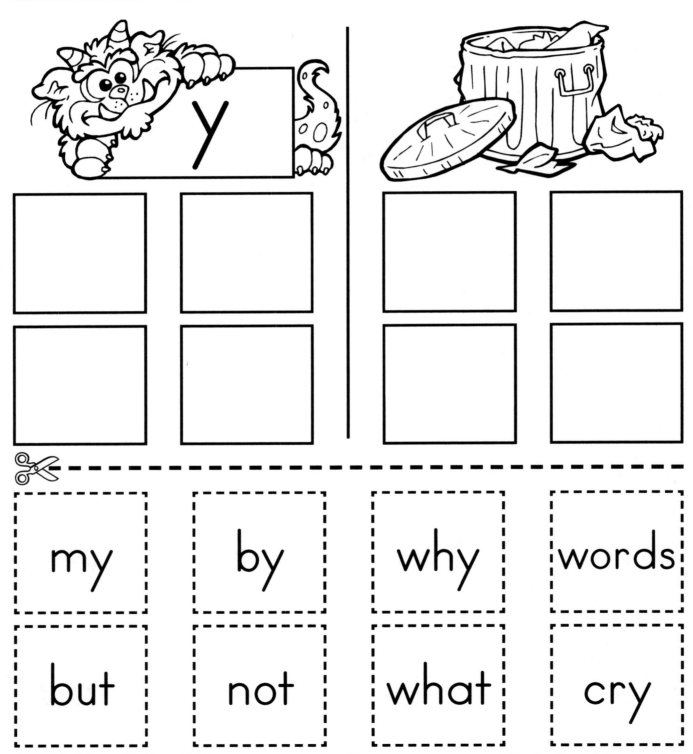

Schwa Sounds

Phonics Instructions: The schwa sound is the unaccented vowel sound like *a* in *ago*. It is the same sound whether it is made by *a* in *ago* or *o* in *of*. Some dictionaries say that the schwa sound and the short *u* sound are the same. The schwa sound has a fairly high frequency and is important for anyone using phonics. Ask the student to practice the schwa /ə/ sound in isolation. Then read the words aloud with the student repeating them. Have the student sort the words.

Student Directions: Cut out the words at the bottom of the page. Place the words that have the /ə/ sound under the letter *a*. Place the others under the trash can.

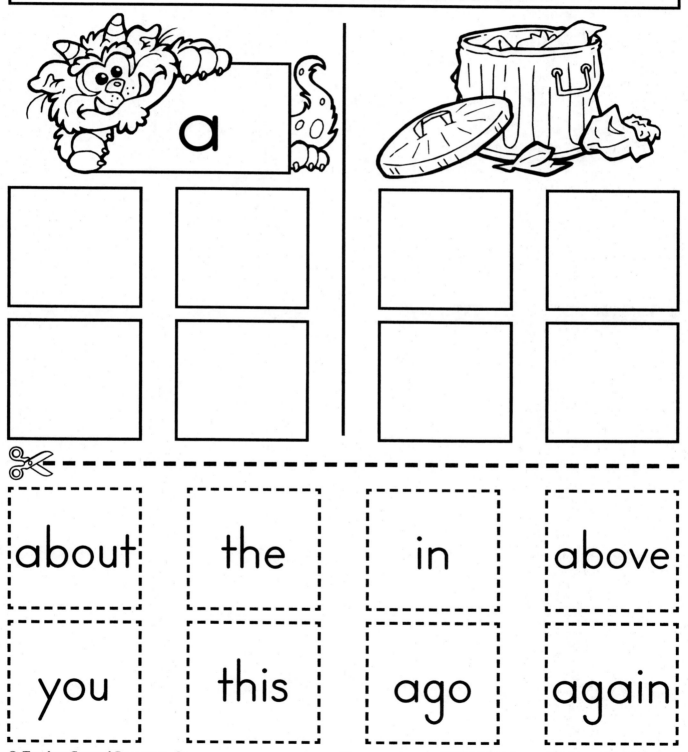

about | the | in | above

you | this | ago | again

Schwa Sounds

Phonics Instructions: The *schwa* sound is the unaccented vowel sound like *e* in *enough*. It is the same sound whether it is made by *a* in *ago*, *e* in *enough*, or *o* in *of*. The schwa sound has a fairly high frequency and is important for anyone using phonics. Ask the student to practice the schwa /ə/ sound in isolation. Then read the words aloud with the student repeating them. Have the student sort the words.

Student Directions: Cut out the words at the bottom of the page. Place the words that have the /ə/ sound under the letter *e*. Place the others under the trash can.

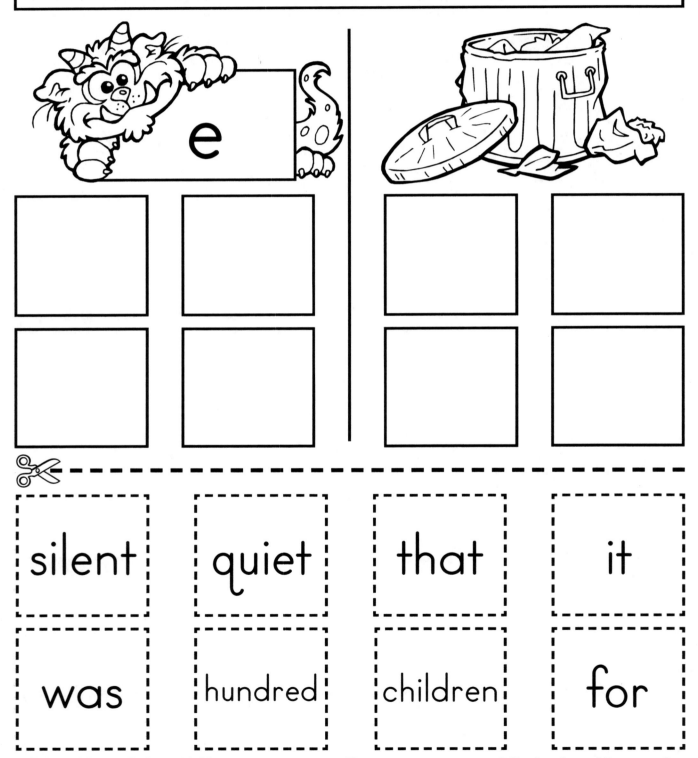

| silent | quiet | that | it |
| was | hundred | children | for |

Schwa Sounds

Phonics Instructions: The schwa sound is the unaccented vowel or short *u* like *o* in *come*. It is the same sound whether it is made by *a* in *ago* or *o* in *of*. The schwa sound has a fairly high frequency and is important for anyone using phonics. Ask the student to practice the schwa /∂/ in isolation. Read the words aloud with the student repeating them.

Student Directions: Cut out the words at the bottom of the page. Place the words that have the /∂/ sound under the letter o. Place the others under the trash can.

other   of   often   are

with   his   they   office

Long Vowel Digraphs

Phonics Instructions: The long *e* sound is sometimes made by the two-letter combination (digraph) *ea*, as in *eat*. This is sometimes referred to as the double vowel rule, but there are so many double vowels that do not make a long vowel sound that it is preferable to pick out only those which do and call them long vowel digraphs. Ask the student to practice the long /ē/ sound in isolation. Then read the words aloud with the student repeating them. Have the student sort the words.

Student Directions: Cut out the words at the bottom of the page. Place the words that have the long /ē/ sound under the letters *ea*. Place the others under the trash can.

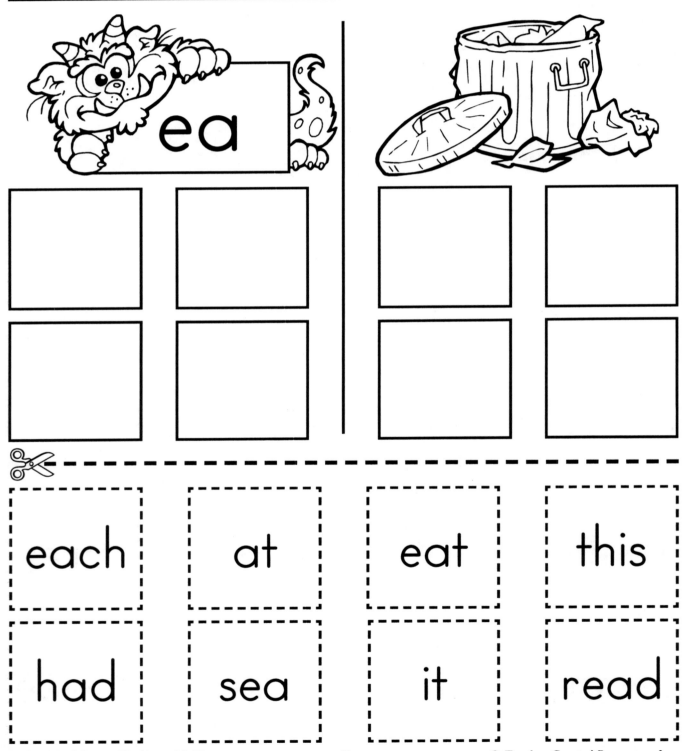

each   at   eat   this

had   sea   it   read

Long Vowel Digraphs

Phonics Instructions: The long *e* sound is also made by the two-letter combination (digraph) *ee*, as in *three*. This is sometimes referred to as the double vowel, but there are so many double vowels that do not make a long vowel sound that it is preferable to pick out only those which do and call them long vowel digraphs. Ask the student to practice the long /ē/ sound in isolation. Then read the words aloud with the student repeating them. Have the student sort the words.

Student Directions: Cut out the words at the bottom of the page. Place the words that have the long /ē/ sound under the letters *ee*. Place the others under the trash can.

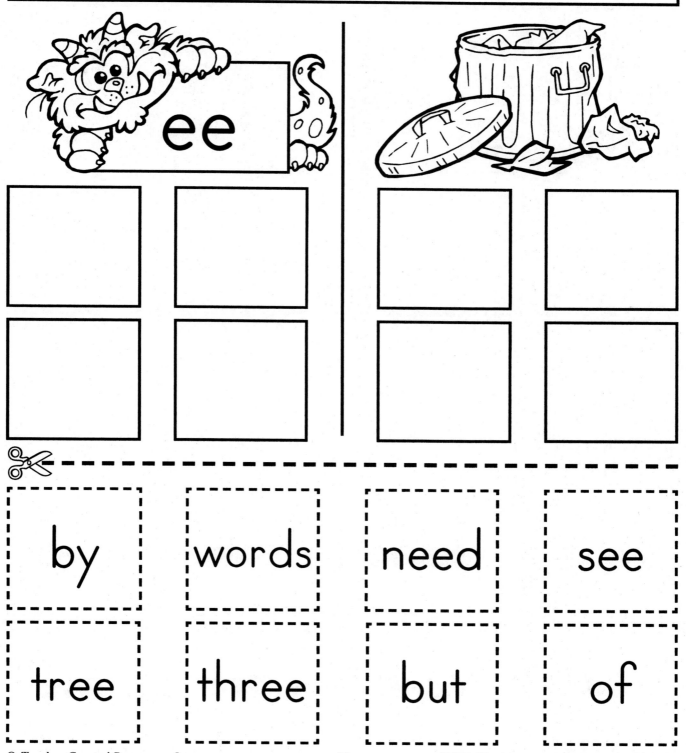

Long Vowel Digraphs

Phonics Instructions: The long *a* sound is sometimes made by the two-letter combination (digraph) *ai*, as in *rain*. This is sometimes referred to as the double vowel rule, but there are so many double vowels that do not make a long vowel sound that it is preferable to pick out only those which do and call them long vowel digraphs. Ask the student to practice the long /ā/ sound in isolation. Then read the words aloud with the student repeating them. Have the student sort the words.

Student Directions: Cut out the words at the bottom of the page. Place the words that have the long /ā/ sound under the letters *ai*. Place the others under the trash can.

Long Vowel Digraphs

Phonics Instructions: The long *a* sound is also made by the two-letter combination (digraph) *ay*, as in *day*. Ask the student to practice the long /ā/ sound in isolation. Then read the words aloud with the student repeating them. Have the student sort the words.

Student Directions: Cut out the words at the bottom of the page. Place the words that have the long /ā/ sound under the letters *ay*. Place the others under the trash can.

ay

play   the   of   day

say   may   and   to

Long Vowel Digraphs

Phonics Instructions: The long *o* sound is sometimes made by the two-letter combination (digraph) *oa*, as in *coat*. This is sometimes referred to as the double vowel rule, but there are so many double vowels that do not make a long vowel sound that it is preferable to pick out only those which do and call them long vowel digraphs. Ask the student to practice the long /ō/ sound in isolation. Then read the words aloud with the student repeating them. Have the student sort the words.

Student Directions: Cut out the words at the bottom of the page. Place the words that have the long /ō/ sound under the letters *oa*. Place the others under the trash can.

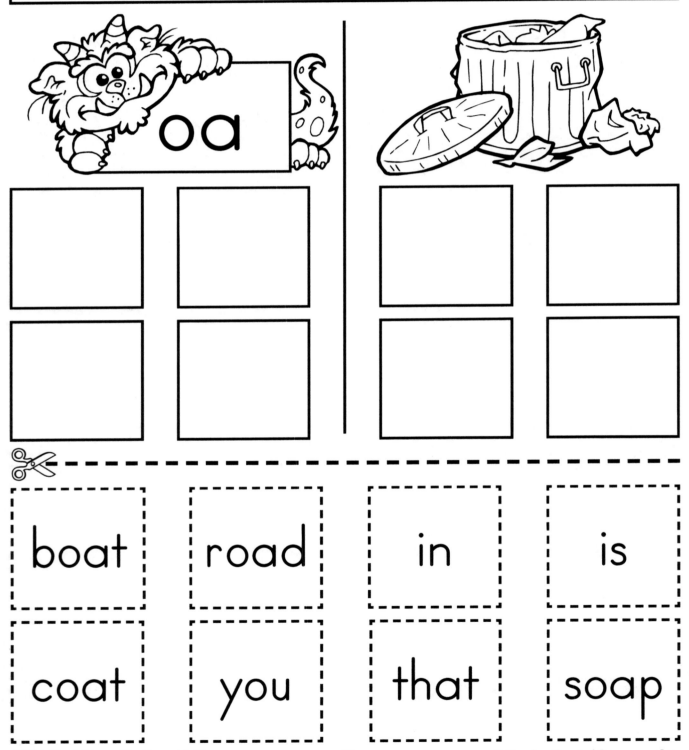

boat   road   in   is

coat   you   that   soap

Long Vowel Digraphs

Phonics Instructions: The long *o* sound is also sometimes made by the two-letter combination (digraph) *ow*, as in *show*. Ask the student to practice the long /ō/ sound in isolation. Then read the words aloud with the student repeating them. Have the student sort the words.

Student Directions: Cut out the words at the bottom of the page. Place the words that have the long /ō/ sound under the letters *ow*. Place the others under the trash can.

Vowel Plus R

Phonics Instructions: The letter combination *or* makes the sound heard in *or* or *for*. Ask the student to practice the long /ôr/ sound in isolation. Then read the words aloud with the student repeating them. Have the student sort the words.

Student Directions: Cut out the words at the bottom of the page. Place the words that have the long /ôr/ sound under the letters *or*. Place the others under the trash can.

of   and   for   force

in   that   form   forest

Vowel Plus R

Phonics Instructions: The letter combination *ar* makes two sounds. The first sound is *ar*, as in *care*. It is a combination of short *e* /e/ plus *r* /r/. Ask the student to practice the /er/ sound in isolation. Then read the words aloud with the student repeating them. Have the student sort the words.

Student Directions: Cut out the words at the bottom of the page. Place the words that have the /er/ sound under the letters *ar*. Place the others under the trash can.

care   his   rare   share

aware   they   at   this

Vowel Plus R

Phonics Instructions: The letter combination *ar* makes two sounds. The second sound is /är/, as in *far*. Ask the student to practice the /är/ sound in isolation. Then read the words aloud with the student repeating them. Have the student sort the words.

Student Directions: Cut out the words at the bottom of the page. Place the words that have the /är/ sound under the letters *ar*. Place the others under the trash can.

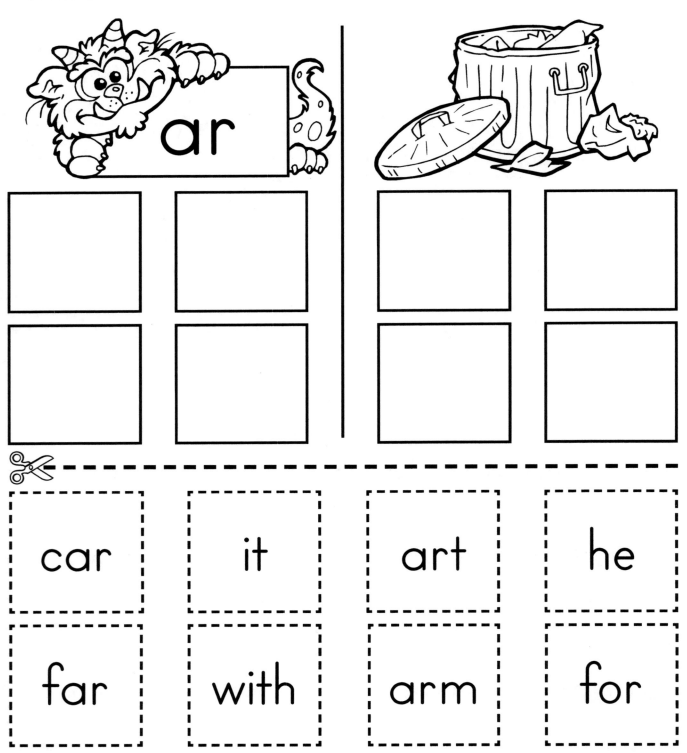

Phonics Instructions: The letter combination *er* makes the sound by the *er* in *her*. It is a combination of short *u* /u/ plus *r* /r/. Ask the student to practice the /ər/ sound in isolation. Then read the words aloud with the student repeating them. Have the student sort the words.

Student Directions: Cut out the words at the bottom of the page. Place the words that have the /ər/ sound under the letters *er*. Place the others under the trash can.

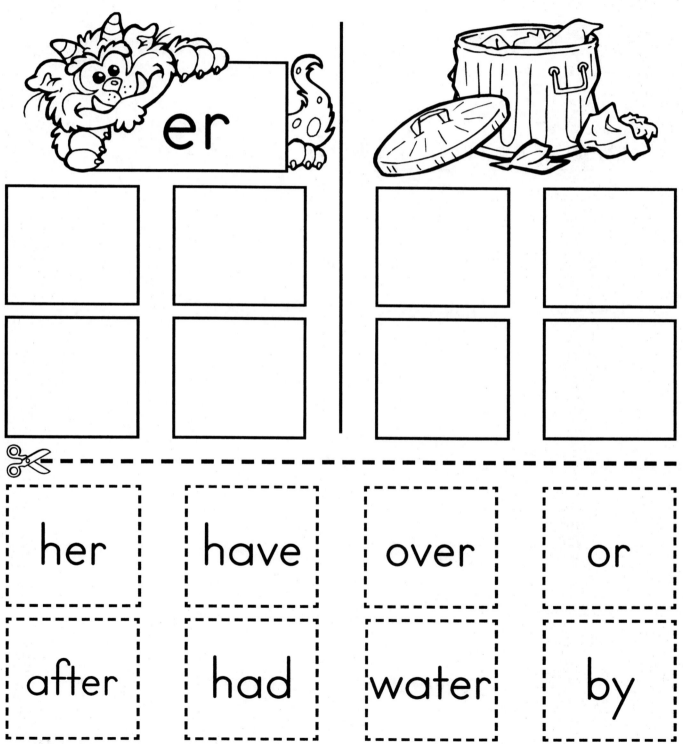

| her | have | over | or |
| after | had | water | by |

Vowel Plus R

Phonics Instructions: The letter combination *ir* makes the sound made by the *ir* in *girl*. It is a combination of short *u* /u/ plus *r* /r/. Ask the student to practice the /∂r/ sound in isolation. Then read the words aloud with the student repeating them. Have the student sort the words.

Student Directions: Cut out the words at the bottom of the page. Place the words that have the /∂r/ sound under the letters *ir*. Place the others under the trash can.

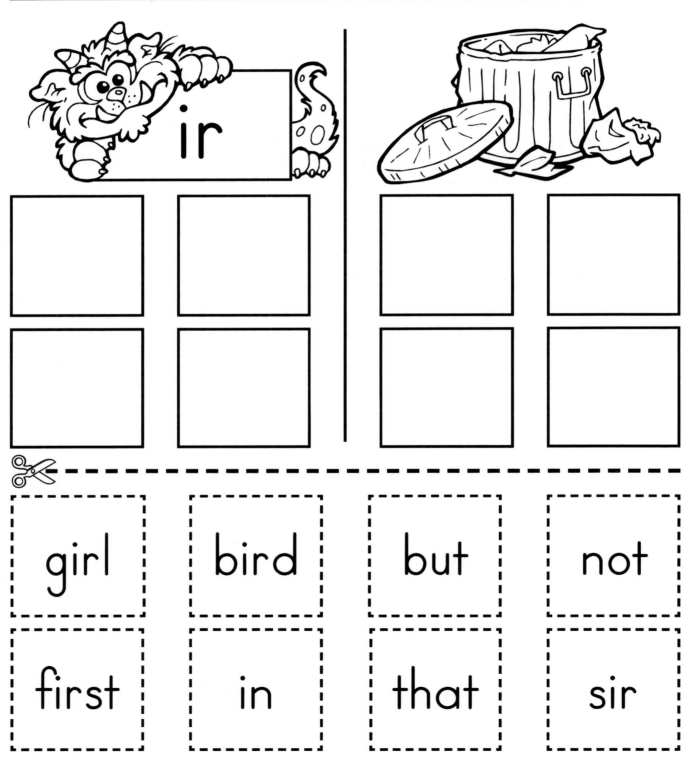

girl   bird   but   not

first   in   that   sir

Vowel Plus R

Phonics Instructions: The letter combination *ur* makes the sound made by *ur* in *turn*. It is a combination of short *u* /u/ plus *r* /r/. Ask the student to practice the /ər/ sound in isolation. Then read the words aloud with the student repeating them. Have the student sort the words.

Student Directions: Cut out the words at the bottom of the page. Place the words that have the /ər/ sound under the letters *ur*. Place the others under the trash can.

burn but church fur

turn not in all

Broad O

Phonics Instructions: The broad *o* sound, as in *off*, is frequently made by the letter *o*. It is often made by *a* in combination with *l*, *u*, or *w*. Ask the student to practice the /ô/ sound in isolation. Then read the words aloud with the student repeating them. Have the student sort the words.

Student Directions: Cut out the words at the bottom of the page. Place the words that have the /ô/ sound under the letter *o*. Place the others under the trash can.

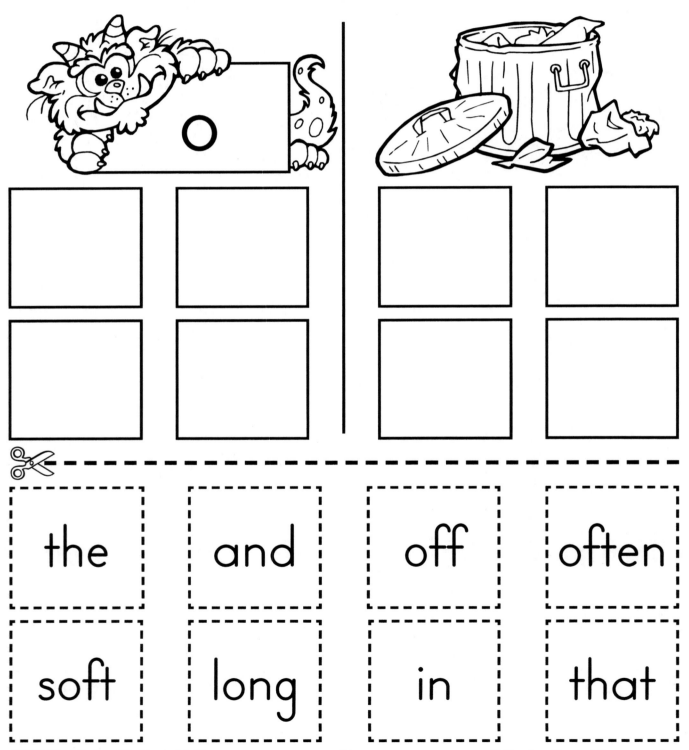

the   and   off   often

soft   long   in   that

Broad O

Phonics Instructions: The broad *o* sound, as in *off*, is frequently made by the letter *o*. It is also made by *a* in combination with *l*, *u*, or *w*. Ask the student to practice the /ôl/ sound in isolation. Then read the words aloud with the student repeating them. Have the student sort the words.

Student Directions: Cut out the words at the bottom of the page. Place the words that have the /ôl/ sound under the letters *al*. Place the others under the trash can.

always   also   it   already

he   was   for   all

Broad O

Phonics Instructions: The broad *o* sound is frequently made by *a* followed by *w*, as in *awful*. Ask the student to practice the /ô/ sound in isolation. Then read the words aloud with the student repeating them. Have the student sort the words.

Student Directions: Cut out the words at the bottom of the page. Place the words that have the /ô/ sound under the letters *aw*. Place the others under the trash can.

Broad O

Phonics Instructions: The broad *o* sound is also frequently made by *a* followed by *u*, as in *auto*. Ask the student to practice the /ô/ sound in isolation. Then read the words aloud with the student repeating them. Have the student sort the words.

Student Directions: Cut out the words at the bottom of the page. Place the words that have the /ô/ sound under the letters *au*. Place the others under the trash can.

Diphthongs

Phonics Instructions: The diphthong sound /ou/ is usually made by the letters *ou*, as in *out*. Ask the student to practice the /ou/ sound in isolation. Then read the words aloud with the student repeating them. Have the student sort the words.

Student Directions: Cut out the words at the bottom of the page. Place the words that have the /ou/ sound under the letters *ou*. Place the others under the trash can.

Diphthongs

Phonics Instructions: The dipthong sound /ou/, as in *out*, is also made by *ow*, as in *cow*. Ask the student to practice the /ou/ sound in isolation. Then read the words aloud with the student repeating them. Have the student sort the words.

Student Directions: Cut out the words at the bottom of the page. Place the words that have the /ou/ sound under the letters *ow*. Place the others under the trash can.

ow

words | but | what | how

now | cows | down | all

Diphthongs

Phonics Instructions: The diphthong sound /oi/ is usually made by the letters *oi*, as *oil*. Ask the student to practice the /oi/ sound in isolation. Then read the words aloud with the student repeating them. Have the student sort the words.

Student Directions: Cut out the words at the bottom of the page. Place the words that have the /oi/ sound under the letters *oi*. Place the others under the trash can.

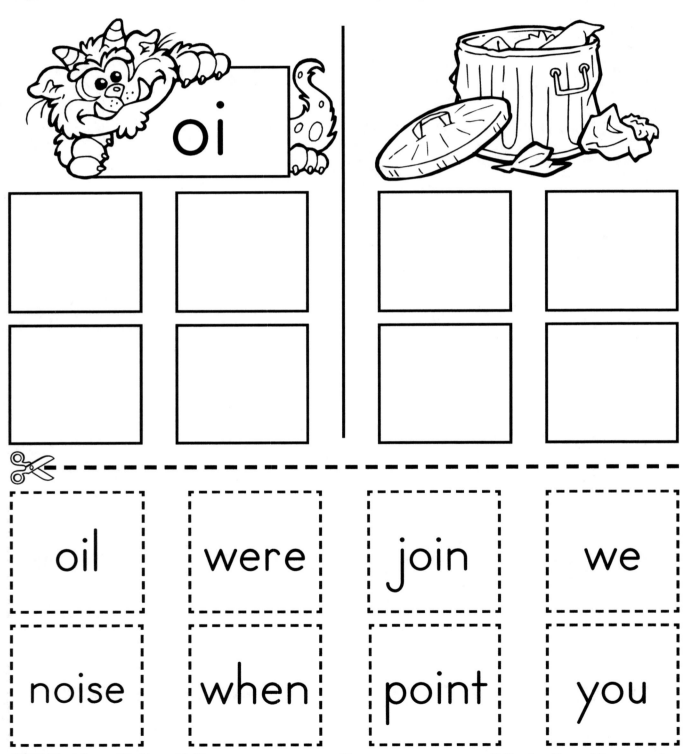

oi

oil | were | join | we

noise | when | point | you

Phonics Instructions: The diphthong sound /oi/ is also made by *oy*, as in *boy*. Ask the student to practice the /oi/ sound in isolation. Then read the words aloud with the student repeating them. Have the student sort the words.

Student Directions: Cut out the words at the bottom of the page. Place the words that have the /oi/ sound under the letters *oy*. Place the others under the trash can.

boy   enjoy   the   toy

of   and   in   destroy

Difficult Vowels

Phonics Instructions: The letter combination *oo* has two sounds, as seen in the words *moon* and *book*. The so-called long sound, or two-dot *u* sound, as in *moon*, is the most common. Ask the student to practice the long /o͞o/ sound in isolation. Then read the words aloud with the student repeating them. Have the student sort the words.

Student Directions: Cut out the words at the bottom of the page. Place the words that have the long /o͞o/ sound under the letters *oo*. Place the others under the trash can.

| moon | that | it | he |
| school | are | soon | room |

Difficult Vowels

Phonics Instructions: The second sound of the letter combination *oo* is the so-called short *oo* or one-dot *u* sound, as in the word *look*. Ask the student to practice the short /ŏŏ/ sound in isolation. Then read the words aloud with the student repeating them. Have the student sort the words.

Student Directions: Cut out the words at the bottom of the page. Place the words that have the short /ŏŏ/ sound under the letters *oo*. Place the others under the trash can.

was | book | for | look

are | foot | as | good

Difficult Vowels

Phonics Instructions: The sound of *u*, as in *rule*, is sometimes called the long *oo* or two-dot *u* sound and is the same sound made by *moon*. Ask the student to practice the long /$\overline{oo}$/ sound in isolation. Then read the words aloud with the student repeating them. Have the student sort the words.

Student Directions: Cut out the words at the bottom of the page. Place the words that have the long /$\overline{oo}$/ sound under the letter *u*. Place the others under the trash can.

| ruler | or | truth | had |
| flute | by | June | words |

Difficult Vowels

Phonics Instructions: The sound of *u*, as in *put*, is sometimes called the short *oo* or one-dot *u* sound, and is the same sound made by *oo* in *look*. Ask the student to practice the short /o͝o/ sound in isolation. Then read the words aloud with the student repeating them. Have the student sort the words.

Student Directions: Cut out the words at the bottom of the page. Place the words that have the short /o͝o/ sound under the letter *u*. Place the others under the trash can.

put

not

full

what

bush

all

were

pulled

Difficult Vowels

Phonics Instructions: The short *e* is sometimes made by the letter combination *ea*, as in *head*. Ask the student to practice the short /e/ sound in isolation. Then read the words aloud with the student repeating them. Have the student sort the words.

Student Directions: Cut out the words at the bottom of the page. Place the words that have the short /e/ sound under the letters *ea*. Place the others under the trash can.

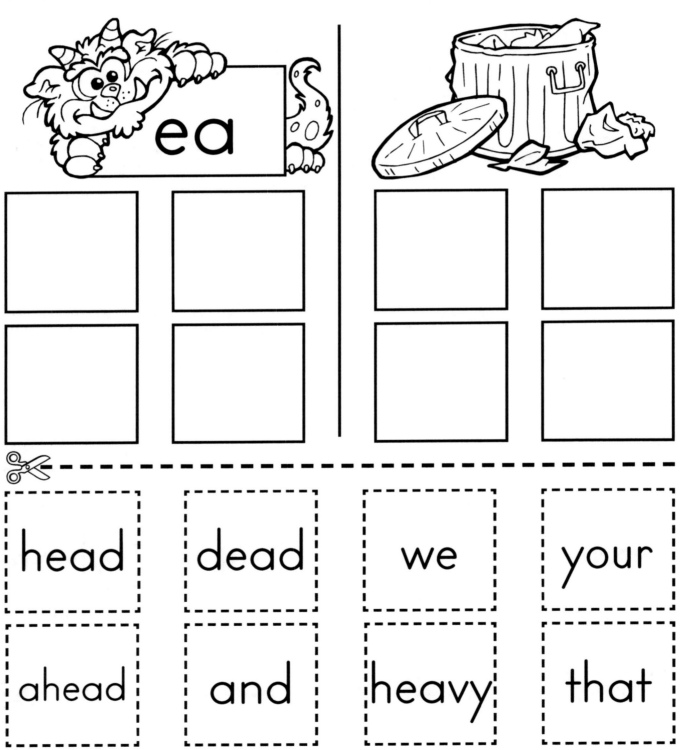

head   dead   we   your

ahead   and   heavy   that

Beginning Consonant Blends

Phonics Instructions: The letter combination *bl* is a consonant blend of two consonant sounds. Ask the student to practice the /bl/ sound in isolation. Then read the name of each picture: blanket, jacket, block, dime, bleach, kite, blouse, zipper. Have the student sort the pictures.

Student Directions: Cut out the pictures at the bottom of the page. Place the pictures that have the /bl/ sound under the letters *bl*. Place the others under the trash can.

Beginning Consonant Blends

Phonics Instructions: The letter combination *cl* is a consonant blend of two consonant sounds. Ask the student to practice the /cl/ sound in isolation. Then read the name of each picture: gum, clock, mop, clothes, hat, cloud, zebra, clown. Have the student sort the pictures.

Student Directions: Cut out the pictures at the bottom of the page. Place the pictures that have the /cl/ sound under the letters *cl*. Place the others under the trash can.

Phonics Instructions: The letter combination *fl* is a consonant blend of two consonant sounds. Ask the student to practice the /fl/ sound in isolation. Then read the name of each picture: flower, flag, hand, horse, queen, kangaroo, flashlight, fly. Have the student sort the pictures.

Student Directions: Cut out the pictures at the bottom of the page. Place the pictures that have the /fl/ sound under the letters *fl*. Place the others under the trash can.

Beginning Consonant Blends

Phonics Instructions: The letter combination *gl* is a consonant blend of two consonant sounds. Ask the student to practice the /gl/ sound in isolation. Then read the name of each picture: glass, shell, globe, zipper, woman, glue, penny, glove. Have the student sort the pictures.

Student Directions: Cut out the pictures at the bottom of the page. Place the pictures that have the /gl/ sound under the letters *gl*. Place the others under the trash can.

Beginning Consonant Blends

Phonics Instructions: The letter combination *pl* is a consonant blend of two consonant sounds. Ask the student to practice the /pl/ sound in isolation. Then read the name of each picture: planets, plant, mop, gum, plate, plus, horse, tree. Have the student sort the pictures.

Student Directions: Cut out the pictures at the bottom of the page. Place the pictures that have the /pl/ sound under the letters *pl*. Place the others under the trash can.

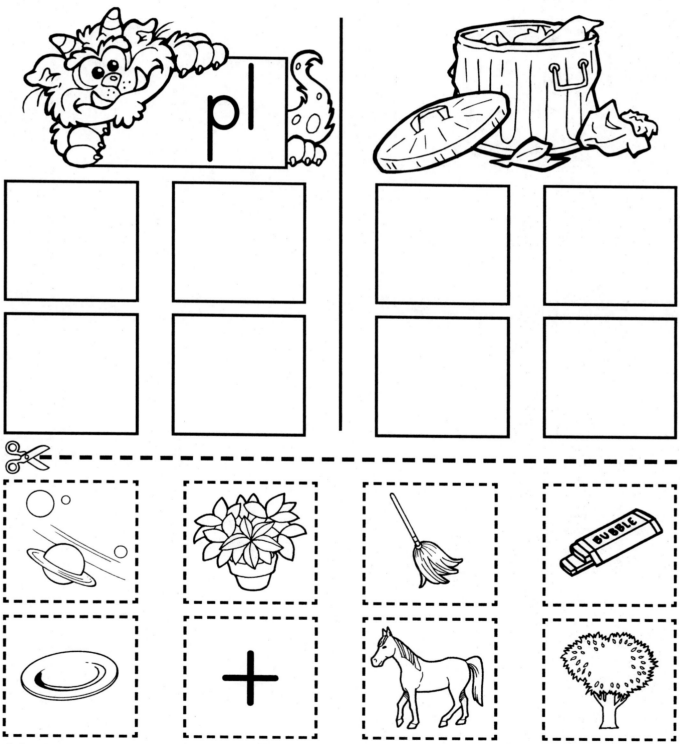

Beginning Consonant Blends

Phonics Instructions: The letter combination *sl* is a consonant blend of two consonant sounds. Ask the student to practice the /sl/ sound in isolation. Then read the name of each picture: sled, queen, slippers, pie, slide, thread, sleep, jacket. Have the student sort the pictures.

Student Directions: Cut out the pictures at the bottom of the page. Place the pictures that have the /sl/ sound under the letters *sl*. Place the others under the trash can.

Beginning Consonant Blends

Phonics Instructions: The letter combination *br* is a consonant blend of two consonant sounds. Ask the student to practice the /br/ sound in isolation. Then read the name of each picture: fan, elephant, bread, broom, brush, bridge, fly, cup. Have the student sort the pictures.

Student Directions: Cut out the pictures at the bottom of the page. Place the pictures that have the /br/ sound under the letters *br*. Place the others under the trash can.

Beginning Consonant Blends

Phonics Instructions: The letter combination *cr* is a consonant blend of two consonant sounds. Ask the student to practice the /cr/ sound in isolation. Then read the name of each picture: yacht, crayons, crown, glass, cracker, book, dog, crab. Have the student sort the pictures.

Student Directions: Cut out the pictures at the bottom of the page. Place the pictures that have the /cr/ sound under the letters *cr*. Place the others under the trash can.

Beginning Consonant Blends

Phonics Instructions: The letter combination *dr* is a consonant blend of two consonant sounds. Ask the student to practice the /dr/ sound in isolation. Then read the name of each picture: lamp, fish, drum, drink, comb, drill, dress, key. Have the student sort the pictures.

Student Directions: Cut out the pictures at the bottom of the page. Place the pictures that have the /dr/ sound under the letters *dr*. Place the others under the trash can.

Phonics Instructions: The letter combination *gr* is a consonant blend of two consonant sounds. Ask the student to practice the /gr/ sound in isolation. Then read the name of each picture: grass, nickel, grasshopper, bell, grapes, grandma, bed, sun. Have the student sort the pictures.

Student Directions: Cut out the pictures at the bottom of the page. Place the pictures that have the /gr/ sound under the letters *gr*. Place the others under the trash can.

Beginning Consonant Blends

Phonics Instructions: The letter combination *pr* is a consonant blend of two consonant sounds. Ask the student to practice the /pr/ sound in isolation. Then read the name of each picture: bag, princess, pray, yarn, prize, kite, top, present. Have the student sort the pictures.

Student Directions: Cut out the pictures at the bottom of the page. Place the pictures that have the /pr/ sound under the letters *pr*. Place the others under the trash can.

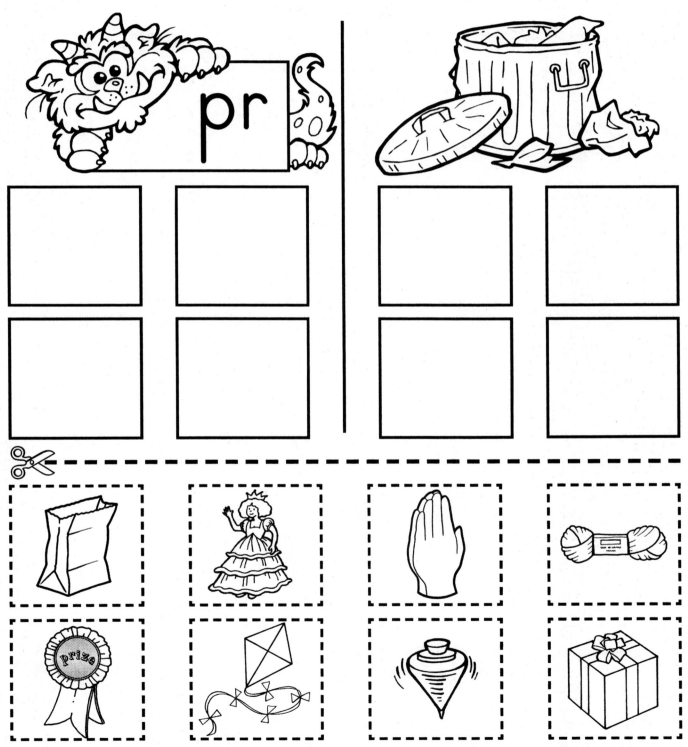

Beginning Consonant Blends

Phonics Instructions: The letter combination *tr* is a consonant blend of two consonant sounds. Ask the student to practice the /tr/ sound in isolation. Then read the name of each picture: tree, ball, pizza, train, truck, eggs, lamp, treasure. Have the student sort the pictures.

Student Directions: Cut out the pictures at the bottom of the page. Place the pictures that have the /tr/ sound under the letters *tr*. Place the others under the trash can.

Beginning Consonant Blends

Phonics Instructions: The letter combination *sc* is a consonant blend of two consonant sounds. Ask the student to practice the /sk/ sound in isolation. Then read the name of each picture: comb, scarf, scorpion, book, vase, screw, scale, jar. Have the student sort the pictures.

Student Directions: Cut out the pictures at the bottom of the page. Place the pictures that have the /sk/ sound under the letters *sc*. Place the others under the trash can.

Beginning Consonant Blends

Phonics Instructions: The letter combination *sk* is a consonant blend of two consonant sounds. Ask the student to practice the /sk/ sound in isolation. Then read the name of each picture: net, log, hat, skirt, skis, skunk, skate, duck. Have the student sort the pictures.

Student Directions: Cut out the pictures at the bottom of the page. Place the pictures that have the /sk/ sound under the letters *sk*. Place the others under the trash can.

Beginning Consonant Blends

Phonics Instructions: The letter combination *sn* is a consonant blend of two consonant sounds. Ask the student to practice the /sn/ sound in isolation. Then read the name of each picture: fire, vest, snowflake, snake, pie, snail, snorkel, yarn. Have the student sort the pictures.

Student Directions: Cut out the pictures at the bottom of the page. Place the pictures that have the /sn/ sound under the letters *sn*. Place the others under the trash can.

Beginning Consonant Blends

Phonics Instructions: The letter combination *sp* is a consonant blend of two consonant sounds. Ask the student to practice the /sp/ sound in isolation. Then read the name of each picture: sponge, tie, spoon, cat, elephant, spaceship, bike, spatula. Have the student sort the pictures.

Student Directions: Cut out the pictures at the bottom of the page. Place the pictures that have the /sp/ sound under the letters *sp*. Place the others under the trash can.

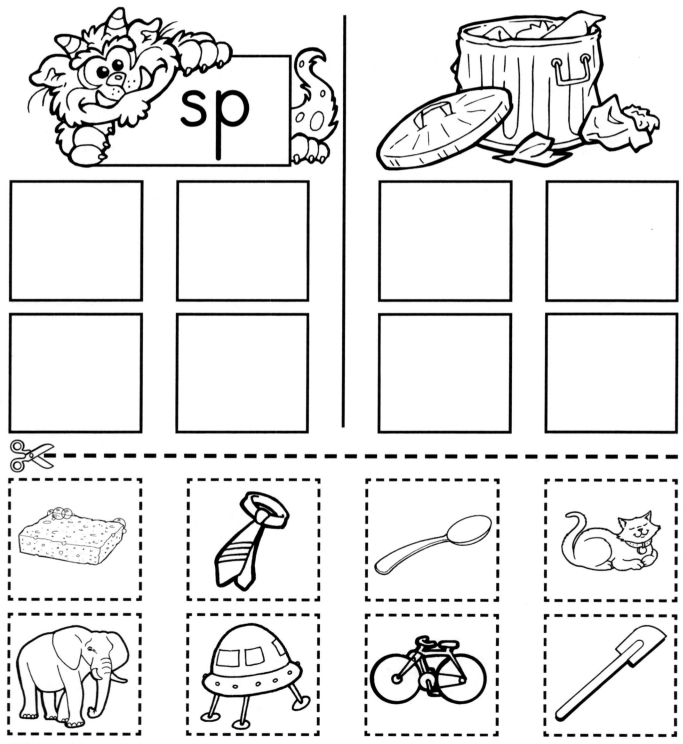

Beginning Consonant Blends

Phonics Instructions: The letter combination *st* is a consonant blend of two consonant sounds. Ask the student to practice the /st/ sound in isolation. Then read the name of each picture: stamp, star, monkey, block, doll, strawberry, boat, stapler. Have the student sort the pictures.

Student Directions: Cut out the pictures at the bottom of the page. Place the pictures that have the /st/ sound under the letters *st*. Place the others under the trash can.

Beginning Consonant Blends

Phonics Instructions: The letter combination *sw* is a consonant blend of two consonant sounds. Ask the student to practice the /sw/ sound in isolation. Then read the name of each picture: bat, sweater, rat, nest, frog, swing, swan, swim. Have the student sort the pictures.

Student Directions: Cut out the pictures at the bottom of the page. Place the pictures that have the /sw/ sound under the letters *sw*. Place the others under the trash can.

Page 4
t: top, train, table, tree
trash: ball, bed, frog, mouse

Page 5
n: nest, 9, nurse, nickel
trash: fish, bat, ring, jam

Page 6
r: rabbit, ruler, rake, radio
trash: fan, pig, lips, wagon

Page 7
m: man, moon, meat, mop
trash: pencil, goat, block, kite

Page 8
d: duck, dress, drum, dog
trash: car, frog, wagon, mask

Page 9
s: sun, saw, sock, star
trash: watch, cat, pig, flower

Page 10
l: lamp, leaf, ladder, letter
trash: key, table, jar, house

Page 11
c: cat, cup, car, cow
trash: rug, vest, ring, glove

Page 12
p: pig, pencil, paint, penny
trash: yarn, fire, brush, vase

Page 13
b: book, box, bell, bowl
trash: snake, pie, wig, mop

Page 14
f: fish, flower, fox, fan
trash: pizza, bird, saw, bag

Page 15
v: vest, vase, van, violin
trash: comb, shoe, cap, tire

Page 16
a: apple, ant, alligator, ax
trash: fish, comb, bell, wig

Page 17
e: elephant, eggs, elbow, elf
trash: moon, duck, cat, sun

Page 18
i: igloo, Indian, insect, ink
trash: lamp, ball, rake, nurse

Page 19
o: ostrich, otter, octopus, oxen
trash: key, wig, fish, bell

Page 20
u: umbrella, underwear, undersea, umpire
trash: kite, fly, moon, vase

Page 21
–y: baby, any, many, very
trash: on, are, with, his

Page 22
–e: one, were, there, come
trash: at, be, this, or

Page 23
a–e: make, made, take, same
trash: one, at, by, words

Page 24
i–e: five, line, side, write
trash: but, not, what, in

Page 25
o–e: bone, home, hope, those
trash: all, were, not, we

Page 26
a: lady, baby, radio, table
trash: glue, bed, gum, pig

Page 27
e: three, equal, tree, beehive
trash: box, cat, car, lamp

Page 28
i: tiger, triangle, bicycle, spider
trash: duck, flag, frog, book

Page 29
o: ocean, potato, piano, radio
trash: bag, skate, net, scale

Page 30
u: ruler, tuba, music, human
trash: be, this, have, or

Page 31
g: grapes, glass, gum, girl
trash: book, pencil, elephant, tire

Page 32
h: horse, hand, home, hat
trash: box, tree, bat, car

Page 33
k: key, kite, king, kangaroo
trash: frog, ring, drum, jam

Page 34
w: woman, wagon, wig, watch
trash: pig, mask, penny, fire

Page 35
j: jam, jacket, jar, jacks
trash: duck, paint, table, mouse

Page 36
x: fox, 6, box, ax
trash: yarn, dog, elephant, igloo

Page 37
qu: queen, quarter, question, quilt
trash: rake, top, fan, bed

Page 38
z: zebra, 0, zipper, zucchini
trash: ring, penny, cup, table

Page 39
y: yarn, yo-yo, yogurt, yacht
trash: shoe, leaf, cap, comb

Page 40
th: that, they, this, there
trash: of, and, to, you

Page 41
th: thimble, thread, 13, thumb
trash: cow, vase, pie, mop

Page 42
ch: chair, cheese, children, cherries
trash: pencil, ladder, bird, snake

Page 43
sh: shirt, sheep, shell, shorts
trash: nickel, lamp, jar, violin

Page 44
wh: wheel, whistle, whale, wheat
trash: apple, book, king, jacket

Page 45
c: cents, city, certain, century
trash: that, it, he, for

Page 46
s: is, as, was, his
trash: on, are, with, they

Page 47
g: gym, giant, genie, germ
trash: at, this, have, had

Page 48
y: my, by, why, cry
trash: words, but, not, what

Page 49
a: about, above, ago, again
trash: the, in, you, this

Page 50
e: silent, quiet, hundred, children
trash: that, it, was, for

Answer Key

Page 51
o: other, of, often, office
trash: are, with, his, they

Page 52
ea: each, eat, sea, read
trash: at, this, had, it

Page 53
ee: need, see, tree, three
trash: by, words, but, of

Page 54
ai: wait, paint, train, main
trash: not, what, were, me

Page 55
ay: play, day, say, may
trash: the, of, and, to

Page 56
oa: boat, road, coat, soap
trash: in, is, you, that

Page 57
ow: own, slow, show, low
trash: it, he, for, was

Page 58
or: for, force, form, forest
trash: of, and, in, that

Page 59
ar: care, rare, share, aware
trash: his, they, at, this

Page 60
ar: car, art, far, arm
trash: it, he, with, for

Page 61
er: her, over, after, water
trash: have, or, had, by

Page 62
ir: girl, bird, first, sir
trash: but, not, in, that

Page 63
ur: burn, church, fur, turn
trash: but, not, in, all

Page 64
o: off, often, soft, long
trash: the, and, in, that

Page 65
al: always, also, already, all
trash: it, he, was, for

Page 66
aw: saw, law, draw, straw
trash: on, ate, with, his

Page 67
au: cause, author, caught, autumn
trash: they, at, be, this

Page 68
ou: out, our, house, hour
trash: had, by, have, it

Page 69
ow: how, now, cows, down
trash: words, but, what, all

Page 70
oi: oil, join, noise, point
trash: were, we, when, you

Page 71
oy: boy, enjoy, toy, destroy
trash: the, of, and, in

Page 72
oo: moon, school, soon, room
trash: that, it, he, are

Page 73
oo: book, look, foot, good
trash: was, for, are, as

Page 74
u: ruler, truth, flute, June
trash: or, had, by, words

Page 75
u: put, full, bush, pulled
trash: not, what, all, were

Page 76
ea: head, dead, ahead, heavy
trash: we, your, and, that

Page 77
bl: blanket, block, bleach, blouse
trash: jacket, dime, kite, zipper

Page 78
cl: clock, clothes, cloud, clown
trash: gum, mop, hat, zebra

Page 79
fl: flower, flag, flashlight, fly
trash: hand, horse, queen,
    kangaroo

Page 80
gl: glass, globe, glue, glove
trash: shell, zipper, woman, penny

Page 81
pl: planets, plant, plate, plus
trash: mop, gum, horse, tree

Page 82
sl: sled, slippers, slide, sleep
trash: queen, pie, thread, jacket

Page 83
br: bread, broom, brush, bridge
trash: fan, elephant, fly, cup

Page 84
cr: crayons, crown, cracker, crab
trash: yacht, glass, book, dog

Page 85
dr: drum, drink, drill, dress
trash: lamp, fish, comb, key

Page 86
gr: grass, grasshopper, grapes,
    grandma
trash: nickel, bell, bed, sun

Page 87
pr: princess, pray, prize, present
trash: bag, yarn, kite, top

Page 88
tr: tree, train, truck, treasure
trash: ball, pizza, eggs, lamp

Page 89
sc: scarf, scorpion, screw, scale
trash: comb, book, vase, jar

Page 90
sk: skirt, skis, skunk, skate
trash: net, log, hat, duck

Page 91
sn: snowflake, snake, snail, snorkel
trash: fire, vest, pie, yarn

Page 92
sp: sponge, spoon, spaceship,
    spatula
trash: tie, cat, elephant, bike

Page 93
st: stamp, star, strawberry, stapler
trash: monkey, block, doll, boat

Page 94
sw: sweater, swing, swan, swim
trash: bat, rat, nest, frog